W9-BWF-467

DATE DUE

The Library of HOLIDAYS™

St. Patrick's Day

Amy Margaret

The Rosen Publishing Group's
PowerKids Press™
New York

For sweet Carly Rose

Published in 2002 by The Rosen Publishing Group, Inc.
29 East 21st Street, New York, NY 10010

First Edition

Book Design: Michael Caroleo and Michael de Guzman
Project Editors: Jennifer Quasha and Joanne Randolph

Photo Credits: p. 4 (St. Patrick's Day postcard) © Bettmann/CORBIS, (map and shamrock background) by Michael de Guzman; p. 7 © Araldo de Luca/CORBIS; p. 8 © Archive Photos; p. 11 © Jack Hollingsworth/CORBIS; p. 12 © Fritz Polking; Frank Lane Picture Agency/CORBIS; p. 15 © Joseph Sohm; ChromoSohm Inc./CORBIS; p. 16 © Becky Luigart-Stayner/CORBIS; p. 19 © Museum of the City of New York/CORBIS; p. 20 © Louis Goldman/FPG International; p. 22 © Joseph Sohm; ChromoSohm Inc./CORBIS

Margaret, Amy.
   St. Patrick's Day / Amy Margaret. — 1st ed.
       p. cm. — (The library of the holidays)
Includes index.
   ISBN 0-8239-5783-7 (lib. bdg.)
1. Saint Patrick's Day—Juvenile literature. [1. Saint Patrick's Day. 2. Holidays] I. Title. II. Series.
   GT4995.P3 M37 2002
   394.262—dc21

                                            00-012196

Manufactured in the United States of America

Contents

St. Patrick's Day Greetings

IRELAND

Ireland's Spring Holiday

Each year on March 17, people around the world celebrate St. Patrick's Day. It is an important holiday both in the United States and in Ireland. This holiday brings together Irish people. St. Patrick's Day is **celebrated** to remind us of the good deeds done by a generous **Christian** man named Patrick. He spent most of his life sharing his Christian beliefs with the people of Ireland. We honor Patrick and his contributions to Ireland on the date of his death, March 17.

◀ *This is a map of Ireland, where Saint Patrick did his good deeds. Behind the map, a greeting card shows Patrick surrounded by shamrocks, a traditional symbol of St. Patrick's Day.*

5

Patrick, the Boy

Patrick was born in England around A.D. 385. When Patrick was 16, pirates kidnapped him and took him to Ireland. A landowner bought Patrick to be his slave. For six lonely years, Patrick watched over his master's sheep. His only comfort was prayer. One day, a voice told him to run away. He felt he had heard God's voice. He went to the coast and found work on a ship that was about to sail. Patrick did not want to work on the ship forever, though. He wanted to **devote** his life to God.

Patrick spent many lonely hours in the field watching his master's sheep. The quiet setting gave him time to pray. ▶

Patrick, the Missionary

After his escape, Patrick became educated in Europe. In England, he heard God speak to him again. Patrick was told to go back to Ireland to teach the people about the Christian **faith**. Most Irish people followed **pagan** priests, called **druids**. The druids worshiped gods of nature and used magic. Patrick traveled to villages and taught about the Bible and God. Some people did not like his work. They tried to beat or kill him. They failed, and he continued his work for 30 or 40 years.

St. Patrick shows the Irish people the book of the four gospels. He wanted people to read the Bible and love God like he did.

Saint Patrick, the Saint of Ireland

Around the year A.D. 461, Patrick died in Saul, Ireland, where he built his first church. The Irish loved him so much that they made him a **Catholic** saint. He became Saint Patrick. Saint Patrick is honored in Ireland, Belgium, France, Italy, and the United States. Many churches are named after him. Saint Patrick chose Armagh, Ireland, as the home for his church. Armagh has two churches dedicated to Saint Patrick. One is a **Protestant** church. The other is a Catholic cathedral.

St. Patrick's Cathedral in New York City is just one of many churches that honor the memory of Saint Patrick.

The Shamrock

The **shamrock** is an important **symbol** of St. Patrick's Day. This plant has three leaves and grows all over Ireland. Saint Patrick used the shamrock to explain the **Trinity** to the Irish. The three leaves on the shamrock stand for the Father, Son, and Holy Ghost. The stem shows how the three different beings are united into one. The **tradition** of pinning a shamrock to one's clothing for St. Patrick's Day started in 1681. It still carries on today in Ireland and all over the world!

◀ *The three-leafed shamrock has become a popular symbol of St. Patrick's Day all over the world.*

Other Symbols of St. Patrick's Day

The color green is often connected with Ireland and St. Patrick's Day. It has been Ireland's national color since the nineteenth century. The **leprechaun** is also a symbol of St. Patrick's Day. In Ireland, a leprechaun is a type of fairy. Today we think of leprechauns as small, cheerful men dressed in green. In Ireland, the leprechaun of long ago was much different. He lived alone and was mean to others. Over time, Irish folktales of leprechauns became linked to St. Patrick's Day.

This person has dressed as a leprechaun to celebrate St. Patrick's Day. ▶

A St. Patrick's Day Feast

Potatoes always have been a popular food in Ireland because this crop grows easily in the rich, moist soil. **Colcannon** is a favorite potato dish served on St. Patrick's Day. It is made of mashed potatoes, cut-up cabbage, onion, and melted butter. In America, many people eat corned beef and cabbage on St. Patrick's Day. Irish stew and Irish soda bread are also favorites. In both Ireland and America, people gather on St. Patrick's Day to enjoy these simple, traditional foods.

◀ *To celebrate their Irish heritage, people often eat traditional Irish foods on St. Patrick's Day, such as corned beef, cabbage, and potatoes.*

St. Patrick's Day in Early America

Some of the earliest **immigrants** to arrive in America were Irish. In the 1700s, a group called the Charitable Irish Society was formed in Boston. This group was the first to celebrate St. Patrick's Day in the United States, on March 17, 1737. The popularity of the day grew quickly. Each year, Irish immigrants gathered in taverns to honor Saint Patrick on this day. They spent time drinking and enjoying the company of other Irish people. Today people all over the United States enjoy this special day.

Ever since 1737, the Irish people in America have celebrated St. Patrick's Day. This picture shows a St. Patrick's Day parade in New York City's Union Square during the 1800s. ▶

St. Patrick's Day in America

March 17 has become a widely celebrated day in the United States. The St. Patrick's Day parade in New York City is one of the largest in America. New York City has held this parade each year since about 1762. This holiday is celebrated with parades in most of the 50 states. March 17 is also a popular day for parties. People play Irish music and eat Irish food. Adults and children alike love to celebrate by wearing something green. Some people also pin shamrocks to their clothing.

◀ *These people are marching in New York City's St. Patrick's Day parade. New York City has the largest St. Patrick's Day parade in America.*

St. Patrick's Day in Ireland

St. Patrick's Day was celebrated as a religious holiday when it was first observed in Ireland. As time passed, the holiday grew more festive. After spending the morning in church, some gathered in inns to drink and dance. Dublin, a large city in East Ireland, began hosting its own parade in the 1970s. In recent years, the Irish government has once again stressed the religious side of the holiday. St. Patrick's Day honors an important man who helped to shape Ireland. It is also a time when Irish people celebrate their rich past.

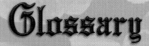

Glossary

Catholic (KATH-lik) Someone who belongs to the Roman Catholic religion.

celebrated (SEH-luh-bray-ted) To be observed as a special time or day with festive activities.

Christian (KRIS-chun) A follower of the teachings of Jesus Christ and the Bible.

colcannon (kuhl-KA-nuhn) An Irish dish of mashed potatoes, onions, cabbage, and butter.

devote (dih-VOHT) To commit.

druids (DROO-idz) Believers in an ancient religion from northern Europe.

faith (FAYTH) A belief without proof.

immigrants (IH-mih-grints) People who have moved to a new country from another country.

leprechaun (LEP-ruh-kon) A type of fairy from Irish folklore.

pagan (PAY-gen) Not Christian.

Protestant (PRAH-tus-tent) A follower of a religion based on Christian beliefs.

shamrock (SHAM-rahk) A three-leafed plant found in Ireland.

symbol (SIM-bul) An object or a design that stands for something important.

tradition (truh-DIH-shun) A way of doing something that is passed down through the years.

Trinity (TRIH-neh-tee) The Christian idea that the Father, Son, and Holy Ghost are three different beings, but also one.

23

Index

B
Bible, 9

C
Catholic, 10
Charitable Irish
    Society, 18
Christian, 5, 9
church, 10, 22
colcannon, 17

D
druids, 9

F
folktales, 14
food, 17

G
God, 6, 9
green, 14, 21

L
leprechaun, 14

P
pagan, 9
parade, 21
potatoes, 17
prayer, 6
Protestant, 10

R
religious, 22

S
shamrock(s), 13,
    21

T
taverns, 18
tradition, 13
Trinity, 13

Web Sites

Due to the changing nature of Internet links, PowerKids Press has developed an online list of Web sites related to the subject of this book. This site is updated regularly. Please use this link to access the list:
www.powerkidslinks.com/lhol/saintp/